Janice VanCleave's
WILD, WACKY, and WEIRD
Science Experiments

Janice VanCleave's
Wild, Wacky, and Weird
EARTH SCIENCE EXPERIMENTS

ROSEN
PUBLISHING

New York

This edition published in 2017 by:
The Rosen Publishing Group, Inc.
29 East 21st Street
New York, NY 10010

Library of Congress Cataloging-in-Publication Data

Names: VanCleave, Janice Pratt.
Title: Janice VanCleave's wild, wacky, and weird earth science experiments /
  Janice VanCleave.
Description: New York : Rosen Central, 2016. | Series: Janice VanCleave's
  wild, wacky, and weird science experiments | Audience: Grades 5-8. |
  Includes bibliographical references and index.
Identifiers: LCCN 2016009078| ISBN 9781477789759 (library bound) | ISBN
  9781477789735 (pbk.) | ISBN 9781477789742 (6-pack)
Subjects: LCSH: Earth sciences--Experiments--Juvenile literature. | Science
  projects--Juvenile literature.
Classification: LCC QE29 .V363 2016 | DDC 550.78--dc23
LC record available at https://lccn.loc.gov/2016009078

Manufactured in China

Experiments first published in *Janice VanCleave's 202 Oozing, Bubbling, Dripping, and Bouncing Experiments* by John Wiley & Sons, Inc. copyright © 1996 Janice VanCleave.

CONTENTS

Introduction...4

Megaweight 8

Rainbow..10

Dripper...12

Gulp! 14

Fossil Dig 16

Ticker 18

Shifting 20

Pop Top 22

Widening 24

Squeezed 26

Jolted 28

Bang! 30

S-Waves..32

Side-to-Side..34

Tilting 36

Riser..38

Spud Launcher 40

Fire Rocks 42

Squirt! 44

Wash Away 46

Shaping 48

Weathering 50

Speedy..52

Wander 54

Glossary 56

For More Information................................58

For Further Reading.................................60

Index..62

INTRODUCTION

Earth science is the study of earth. Geology is one main area of earth science that deals with the study of the physical planet earth. But oceanography, meteorology, and astronomy are also areas of earth science.

The people who choose earth science as a career do a variety of work. Some work in laboratories and some work outdoors in the field. They study soil, fossils, volcanoes, and earthquakes. All these people have something in common: They are constantly asking questions to learn even more about our planet.

This book is a collection of science experiments about earth science. How does the sun's position affect how a rainbow is made? How do fossils become embedded in ice? How is sound used to find petroleum? You will find the answers to these and many other questions by doing the experiments in this book.

HOW TO USE THIS BOOK

Before you get started, be sure to read each experiment completely. The following sections are included for all the experiments.

» **PURPOSE:** *The basic goals for the experiment.*

» **MATERIALS:** *A list of supplies you will need.*

You will experience less frustration and more fun if you gather all the necessary materials for the experiments before you begin. You lose your train of thought when you have to shop and search for supplies.

» **PROCEDURE:** *Step-by-step instructions on how to perform the experiment.*

Follow each step very carefully, never skip steps, and do not add your own. Safety is of the utmost importance, and by reading the experiment before starting, then following the instructions exactly, you can feel confident that no unexpected results will occur. Ask an adult to help you when you are working with anything sharp or hot. If adult supervisor is required, it will be noted in the experiment.

» **RESULTS:** *An explanation stating exactly what is expected to happen.*

This is an immediate learning tool. If the expected results are achieved, you will know that you did the experiment correctly. If your results are not the same as described in the experiment, carefully read the instructions and start over from the first step.

INTRODUCTION

» **WHY?** *An explanation of why the results were achieved.*

You will be rewarded with successful experiments if you read each experiment carefully, follow the steps in order, and do not substitute materials.

THE SCIENTIFIC METHOD

Scientists identify a problem or observe an event. Then they seek solutions or explanations through research and experimentation. By doing the experiments in this book, you will learn to follow experimental steps and make observations. You will also learn many scientific principles that have to do with earth science.

In the process, the things you see or learn may lead you to new questions. For example, perhaps you have completed the experiment that demonstrates how the speed of running water affects the wearing away of soil. Now you wonder what effect the angle of the water flow would have on this erosion. That's great! Every scientist is curious and asks new questions about what they learn. When you design a new experiment, it is a good idea to follow the scientific method.

1. Ask a question.

2. Do some research about your question. What do you already know?

3. Come up with a hypothesis, or a possible answer to your question.

4. Design an experiment to test your hypothesis. Make sure the experiment is repeatable.

5. Collect the data and make observations.

6. Analyze your results.

7. Reach a conclusion. Did your results support your hypothesis?

Many times the experiment leads to more questions and a new experiment.

Always remember that when devising your own science experiment, have a knowledgeable adult review it with you before trying it out. Ask them to supervise it as well.

MEGAWEIGHT

PURPOSE To demonstrate the difference in the weights of the atmosphere, hydrosphere, and lithosphere.

MATERIALS large paper clip
4-by-12-inch (10-by-30-cm) piece of cardboard
2 rubber bands
pencil
7-ounce (210-ml) paper cup
12-inch (30-cm) piece of string
marking pen
tap water
soil

PROCEDURE

1. Attach the paper clip to the center of one of the short sides of the cardboard. Tie the rubber bands together and hang them on the paper clip.

2. Use the pencil to punch two holes on opposite sides of the cup just under the rim.

3. Loop the string through the rubber band and tie the ends through each hole in the cup.

4. Hold the cardboard so that the cup hangs freely.

5. 5. Let the bottom of the lower rubber band be the pointer. Mark the position of the pointer and label the mark Air.

6. Fill the cup with water. Mark the position of the pointer and label the mark Water.

7. Empty the cup and refill it with soil. Mark the position of the pointer and label the mark Land.

RESULTS Comparing the weight of equal quantities of air, water, and soil indicates that air is the lightest and soil is the heaviest of the three materials.

WHY? The lithosphere is the outer part of the earth, not including the air above the earth (the atmosphere) or the water on the earth (the hydrosphere). This experiment indicates that soil is heavier than air or water.

RAINBOW

PURPOSE To determine how the sun's position affects how a rainbow is made.

MATERIALS garden hose with sprayer

PROCEDURE

NOTE: Since there is a possibility of getting wet, the best time to perform this experiment is on a warm day.

CAUTION: Never look directly at the sun.

1. Turn the water on and adjust the nozzle on the hose so that it sprays a fine mist of water.

2. Stand with the sun behind you and look for a rainbow in the water spray.

3. Turn around so that the sun is in front of you, and look for a rainbow in the water spray, again.

RESULTS A rainbow can be seen only when the sun is behind you.

WHY? A rainbow is an arc of colors in the sky. To see a rainbow, there must be water droplets in the air in front of you and the sun must be shining behind you. When sunlight passes through a raindrop, it is refracted or bent, and the light separates into seven colors: red, orange, yellow, green, blue, indigo, and violet. All rainbows are part of a circle, but only part of the circle is visible because the earth is in the way.

DRIPPER

PURPOSE To demonstrate the formation of stalagmites and stalactites.

MATERIALS 2 baby food jars
Epsom salt
tap water
spoon
2 washers
18-inch (45-cm) piece of cotton string
sheet of dark construction paper

PROCEDURE

NOTE: This activity works best in humid weather.

1. Fill each jar with Epsom salt. Add just enough water to cover the Epsom salt and stir.

2. Tie a washer to each end of the string.

3. Place one washer in each of the jars and place the sheet of paper between the jars.

4. Position the jars so that the string hangs between them with the lowest part of the loop about 1 inch (2.5 cm) above the paper.

5. Allow the jars to stand undisturbed and out of any draft for 1 week or longer.

RESULTS Water drips from the center of the loop onto the paper. A hard, white crust forms on the string and grows down as time passes. A mound of white crystals builds up on the paper beneath the string.

WHY? Water containing Epsom salt moves through the string. As the water evaporates, crystals of Epsom salt are deposited. The Epsom salt formations are models of how crystal deposits form in caves. Stalactites are icicle-shaped crystals that hang from a cave's roof. Stalagmites are crystals that build up from the floor of the cave.

GULP!

PURPOSE To demonstrate one way that fossils become embedded in ice.

MATERIALS cake pan
tap water
heavy rock, about the size of your fist

PROCEDURE

1. Fill the cake pan with water. Place the pan in the freezer overnight to allow the water to freeze.

2. When the water is frozen, leave the pan in the freezer and place the rock on top of the ice.

3. Gently lift the rock once a day for 3 or more days.

RESULTS At first the rock can be lifted, but then it sinks into the ice. The ice sticks to the rock, making it difficult to lift.

WHY? At first the rock is hotter than the ice. The heat of the rock causes the ice to melt, and the rock sinks. After the rock cools, it continues to sink very slowly into the ice. The weight of the rock pushes down on the ice, causing it to melt. The liquid water is cold enough to refreeze around the rock. Fossils (traces of the remains of prehistoric animals and plants) are found deeply embedded in ice, mainly because falling snow covered the organism, but also because the weight of the animal caused it to sink through the ice as the rock did on the pan of ice. The pressure of the organism melted the ice beneath it, and the cold water refroze as the plant or animal sank deeper into the ice.

Gulp!

FOSSIL DIG

PURPOSE To demonstrate how rock can be removed from around a fossil.

MATERIALS paper towel
chocolate-chip cookie
flat toothpick
art brush

PROCEDURE

1. Lay the paper towel on a table.

2. Place the cookie in the center of the paper towel.

3. Follow these steps to remove a chocolate chip from the cookie without scratching the chips or breaking the cookie:

» Use the pointed end of the toothpick to scratch away the cookie around the chocolate chip. Scratch away from the chip and never toward it.

» With the brush, gently brush away the loose pieces of cookie.

RESULTS The chocolate chip is removed from the cookie.

WHY? Fossils found in relatively soft rock can often be removed in a manner similar to the way in which you removed the chocolate chip from the cookie. Instead of a toothpick, an instrument with a metal point is used to flake away rock surrounding the fossil. The rule is always to work away from the fossil. That way, if you slip, only the unwanted rock is scratched and not the fossil. The loosened rock particles are then removed with a stiff-bristled brush.

TICKER

PURPOSE To demonstrate how sound is used to find petroleum.

MATERIALS 2 sheets of printer paper   hardcover book
transparent tape   index card
timer   helper

PROCEDURE

1. Roll and tape the sheets of paper to form two large tubes. Set the timer for 5 or more minutes and place it in the end of one of the tubes.

2. Tape the index card to the table as shown.

3. Position and tape the tubes to the table so that they lie along the sides of the index card with the empty tube extending about 1 inch (2.5 em) past the edge of the table.

4. Place your ear next to the open tube and note the sound of the ticking timer.

5. While listening to the timer, ask your helper to stand the book next to the open ends of the tubes.

RESULTS The ticking is louder with the book in place.

WHY? Sound waves can be reflected off solids, such as the book or rock layers. Scientists are able to determine the type and hardness of rock layers beneath the earth's surface by sending down sound waves and listening to the reflected sound. The hardness of rocks can be determined by the loudness of the reflected sound. Scientists know the hardness of rock where petroleum is found and thus can use this method to find petroleum.

SHIFTING

PURPOSE To demonstrate continental separation.

MATERIALS 2 cups (500 ml) soil
quart (liter) bowl
tap water
spoon
cookie sheet

PROCEDURE

1. Pour the soil into the bowl.

2. Add water and stir until you have a thick mud.

3. Pour the mud onto the cookie sheet.

4. Set the pan of mud in the sun for 2 to 3 days.

5. Push down around the sides of the dried mud.

RESULTS The surface of the dried mud cake cracks.

WHY? The mud is broken into pieces with jagged edges, and all the pieces fit together. The continents of the earth, like the mud cake, look like large jigsaw puzzle pieces. The coastlines of the continents have irregular shapes that appear to fit together. In the past, pressures within the earth may have broken a large land mass into the pieces that now form the separate continents on the earth.

Pop Top

PURPOSE To demonstrate how a geyser works.

MATERIALS large coffee can
tap water
funnel, as tall as the coffee can
1-yard (1-m) piece of plastic tubing

PROCEDURE

1. Fill the can with water.

2. Set the funnel in the can, with the wide end at the bottom.

3. Place the end of the plastic tubing into the water and under the rim of the funnel.

4. Blow into the tubing.

RESULTS Water sprays out the funnel's tube.

WHY? Blowing air under the funnel forces air bubbles up the stem of the funnel. As the air moves upward, it pushes water out the top of the tube. Geysers are inverted funnel-shaped cracks in the earth that are filled by underground streams. When water in the lower part of the crack is heated to boiling, the bubbles of steam rise to the surface. A geyser erupts when water trapped in the neck of the funnel-shaped crack is forced out the top by the rising bubbles of steam. As long as you continue to blow under the funnel, water erupts out the top, but natural geysers erupt only when enough pressure builds up to force the water up and out the top of the crack.

22

Coffee Can

Funnel

Plastic tubing under rim of funnel

WIDENING

PURPOSE To demonstrate the expansion of the Mid-Atlantic Ridge.

MATERIALS scissors
ruler
sheet of printer paper
shoe box
modeling clay

PROCEDURE

1. Cut two 3-by-11-inch (7-by-28-cm) strips from the paper.

2. Cut out a ½-by-3½-inch (1-by-9-cm) slit from the center of the bottom of the shoe box, as shown in the diagram.

3. Cut out a 3-by-6-inch (7.5-by-15-cm) section in the center of one of the box's largest sides.

4. Put the paper strips together, and run them up through the slit in the box. Pull the strips out about 3 inches (7.5 cm), fold them back on opposite sides, and place a piece of clay on the end of each strip.

5. Hold the papers under the box and slowly push the strips up through the slit.

RESULTS The clay pieces move away from each other.

WHY? The clay represents old sea floor bordering the Mid-Atlantic Ridge. The rising paper acts like the hot, molten rock moving out of the crack in the mid-ocean ridge. When liquid rock pushes through the ocean floor's surface, it forms a new layer on both sides of the crack. It is believed that this new material pushes against the old floor, causing it to spread apart.

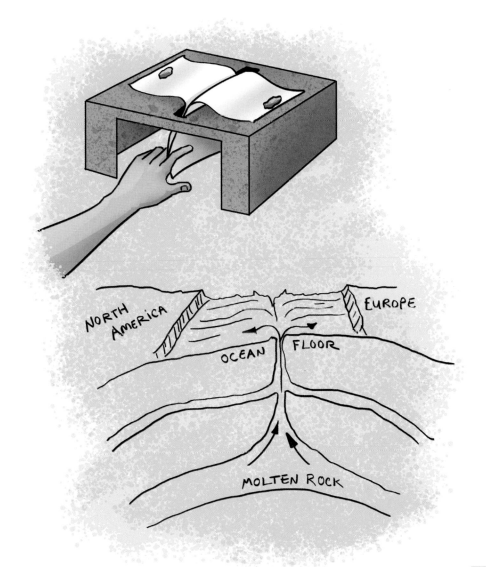

SQUEEZED

PURPOSE To determine how compression forces can bend layers of rock.

MATERIALS 2 large thin sponges
tap water

PROCEDURE

1. Moisten the sponges with water to make them flexible.

2. Lay the moist sponges on top of each other.

3. Place your hands on opposite ends of the sponge "sandwich."

4. While holding the "sandwich" in front of you, slowly push the ends about 2 inches (5 cm) toward the center. The sponge "sandwich" will fold up or down.

5. Repeat step 4, but tilt your hands a little to make the "sandwich" fold in the opposite direction.

RESULTS The sponge "sandwich" folds up and down.

WHY? Pushing from opposite directions causes the sponges to be squeezed into shapes representing folds (bends in rock layers). The result is a surface with a wavelike appearance. Forces pushing toward each other from opposite directions are called compression forces. Compression forces within the earth can crush rocks or can slowly bend rock layers into folds like those of the sponge "sandwich." Folds curving upward are called anticlines and downward curved folds are called synclines.

Squeezed

JOLTED

PURPOSE To determine how faults produce earthquakes.

MATERIALS 2 wooden blocks, each about 2 by 4 by 6 inches (5 by 10 by 15 cm)
2 sheets of medium-grade sandpaper
masking tape

PROCEDURE

1. Wrap each wooden block with a sheet of sandpaper and secure with tape.

2. Hold one block in each hand. The blocks should be held straight up and down.

3. Push the blocks together tightly.

4. While continuing to push the blocks together, try to slide the blocks in different directions.

RESULTS The sandpaper-covered blocks temporarily lock together and then move with a jolt.

WHY? The lithosphere is broken into huge moving pieces referred to as tectonic plates. Where the edges of two plates push against each other, the crack between the plates is called a fault. Friction causes the plates to be temporarily locked together. Faults that are temporarily locked together are called lock faults. The two blocks of wood represent two tectonic plates pushing against each other. They temporarily lock together, but as with actual tectonic plates, the friction between the blocks eventually fails, causing a sudden jolt. The bond holding a locked fault in place is under tremendous stress but may last for years before suddenly slipping. Lock faults inevitably and frequently fail, resulting in an explosion of motion that produces powerful earthquakes (shaking of the earth caused by sudden movement of rock beneath the surface).

PURPOSE To determine how earthquake waves (P-waves) are transmitted through the earth.

MATERIALS
scissors
masking tape
ruler

5 marbles
string

PROCEDURE

1. Cut five 12-inch (30-cm) pieces of string.

2. Tape one string to each of the marbles.

3. Tape the free end of each string to the edge of a table. Adjust the position and length of the strings so that the marbles are at the same height and are side by side.

4. Pull one of the end marbles to the side, and then release it.

5. Observe any movement of the marbles.

RESULTS The marble swings down, striking the closest marble in its path, and stops moving. The marble on the opposite end swings outward and strikes its closest neighboring marble when it swings back into its original position. The cycle of the end marbles swinging back and forth continues for a few seconds.

WHY? The transfer of energy from one marble to the next simulates the movement of energy from the blow of a seismic P-wave (primary earthquake wave) as it travels through the earth's interior. P-waves move through liquids and solids by compressing (pushing together) the material directly in front of them. Each compressed particle quickly springs back to its original position as soon as the energy moves on. The crust (outer layer of the earth's surface) moves upward as it is hit with the energy of the P-wave and then settles back into place when the energy moves on.

Bang!

S-WAVES

PURPOSE To determine how S-waves move through the earth's interior.

MATERIALS 6-foot (2-m) piece of rope

PROCEDURE

1. Tie one end of the rope to a doorknob.

2. Hold the free end of the rope in your hand.

3. Back away from the door until the rope is straight.

4. Gently shake the rope up and down.

5. Gently shake the rope from side to side.

RESULTS Vertical and horizontal S-shaped waves form along the length of the rope.

WHY? Earthquakes produce seismic waves (earthquake vibrations) that move through the body of the earth toward its surface. These seismic waves inside the earth are called body waves. The most energetic and fastest body waves are P-waves, which travel at about 5 miles (8 km) per second. S-waves (secondary waves) are slower body waves that travel at about 2 miles (3.2 km) per second beneath the earth's surface and arrive 5 to 7 minutes after P-waves. Energy from S-waves moves away from the source of vibrations, causing the rock layers to ripple in the same way that the ripples moved along the rope. This up-and-down or side-to-side motion is called a transverse wave.

S-Waves

SIDE-TO-SIDE

PURPOSE To determine how buildings respond to lateral (side-to-side) movements produced by earthquakes.

MATERIALS sheet of coarse (rough) sandpaper
Slinky

PROCEDURE

1. Place the sandpaper on a table.

2. Stand the Slinky on end on the sandpaper.

3. Grab the edge of the sandpaper with your fingers, and quickly pull the paper about 6 inches (15 cm) toward the side of the table.

4. Observe the movement of the Slinky.

RESULTS The bottom of the Slinky is pulled to the side. The top section of the Slinky temporarily lags behind and then springs back into place.

WHY? The bottom of the Slinky is pulled to the side by the movement of the paper beneath it. A similar movement occurs during an earthquake, when the ground below a building moves laterally (sideways). These lateral movements are very destructive, since they cause the walls to bend to one side. Inertia holds the upper part of the Slinky or a building in a leaning position for a fraction of a second, and then the structures snap back into their original shapes. During a typical earthquake lasting only 15 seconds, a building may bend and snap between 15 and 100 times, depending on its structure.

Side-to-Side

TILTING

PURPOSE To determine how a tiltmeter gives clues to when a volcanic eruption is likely to occur.

MATERIALS pencil
two 5-ounce (150-ml) paper cups
drinking straw
modeling clay
shallow baking pan
tap water

PROCEDURE

1. Use the pencil to make a hole through the side of each paper cup near the bottom edge. The holes must be small enough so that the straw will fit tightly.

2. Insert about ½ inch (1.25 cm) of one end of the straw into each hole and seal with the clay.

3. Set the pan on a table and place the connected cups in the center of the pan.

4. Fill both cups half full with water.

5. Lift one end of the pan so that it is about 2 inches (5 cm) above the table. Observe the contents of each cup.

RESULTS Raising the pan causes the amount of water to decrease in the elevated cup and to increase in the lower cup.

WHY? The cups are a model of a tiltmeter (an instrument that measures the tilting of the ground). Volcanologists (scientists who study volcanoes) place the tiltmeter on a volcano, with one end pointing toward the volcano's cone and the other end pointing away. A swelling in the volcano is detected when the water content in the end pointing toward the cone decreases. An unusually large swelling in a short period of time tells scientists that an eruption is most likely on the way.

RISER

PURPOSE To determine how density affects the movement of magma.

MATERIALS tap water
quart (liter) jar with lid
red food coloring
spoon
1 cup (250 ml) vegetable oil
timer

PROCEDURE

1. Pour the water into the jar.

2. Add 10 drops of the food coloring and stir.

3. Slowly add the oil.

4. Secure the lid.

5. Hold the jar so that the light from a window shines through the liquid in the jar.

6. Slowly turn the jar until it is upside down, and then return it to its original position.

7. Observe and record the movement of the contents inside the jar for about 30 seconds.

RESULTS When you first pour the oil into the jar, it floats on top of the colored water. After you tip the jar, most of the oil immediately rises again to rest above the colored water, and small bubbles of oil continue to rise for a short period of time.

WHY? The separation of the two liquids is due to their being immiscible, meaning they do not mix. The differences in the densities (a comparison of the "heaviness" of materials) of the water and oil result in the denser water sinking to the bottom and the less dense oil floating to the top. Like the oil, magma (hot, liquid rock), which is less dense than the rock around it, tends to rise to the surface. Magma begins its upward movement from depths of 35 to 50 miles (56 to 80 km) beneath the earth's crust. This upward journey can be caused by pressures within the earth, but more often magma rises because its density is lower than that of surrounding material.

Spud Launcher

PURPOSE To determine what happens when magma hardens inside a volcano.

MATERIALS knife (to be used only by an adult)
           potato
           2-liter soda bottle
           ½ cup (125 ml) white vinegar
           dish towel
           rubber band
           scissors
           ruler
           bathroom tissue
           1 teaspoon (5 ml) baking soda
           adult helper

PROCEDURE

1. Ask an adult to use the knife to prepare a potato that fits securely as a cork in the bottle.

2. Pour the vinegar into the bottle.

3. For safety, fold the towel around the bottle, leaving only the mouth of the bottle exposed. Secure with the rubber band.

4. Cut a 3-inch (7.5-cm) strip of bathroom tissue and spread the baking soda across its center.

5. Roll the tissue around the baking soda. Secure the packet by twisting the ends of the tissue.

6. Drop the packet of baking soda into the bottle and stopper the bottle with the potato cork.

7. Stand about 1 yard (1 m) away from the bottle and observe.

RESULTS The potato cork pops out of the bottle.

WHY? The baking soda and vinegar mix together, producing carbon dioxide gas. The gas pressure pushes the cork out of the bottle. This experiment can be related to the eruption of a volcano that has a hardened plug of magma in the top of its vent, which prevents gas from bubbling to the sur-face and escaping. As in the bottle, the trapped gas builds up pressure until finally the magma plug is blown out.

Fire Rocks

PURPOSE To determine what type of rock is formed when lava cools.

MATERIALS small box with lid
marbles

PROCEDURE

1. Cover the bottom of the box with a single layer of marbles. The marbles should fit together loosely.

2. Close the lid on the box.

3. Using both hands, lift the box and, while holding the lid secure, shake the box vigorously up and down, then side to side.

4. Quickly set the box on a table, open the lid, and observe the position of the marbles inside.

RESULTS Shaking the box moves the marbles, leaving them in a disorderly arrangement.

WHY? As the temperature of liquid rock within the earth increases, the movement of the molecules in the rock increases. The movement of magma molecules is symbolized in this experiment by the movement of the marbles as the box is shaken. During volcanic eruptions, liquid rock reaches the earth's surface and cools quickly in a matter of days or even hours. Magma that reaches the earth's surface is called lava. This rapid cooling of lava means that the molecules don't have time to move into orderly patterns before the rock solidifies. This produces igneous rock (rock formed from molten rock). (*Igneous* is a Latin word meaning "fire.")

If the rock is formed by the solidification of lava poured out onto the earth's surface, it is called an extrusive igneous rock.

Fire Rocks

SQUIRT!

PURPOSE To demonstrate the action of a shield volcano.

MATERIALS pencil

half-empty tube of toothpaste

PROCEDURE

1. Use the point of a pencil to make a hole in the tube near the cap.

2. Hold the toothpaste tube in your hands.

3. With the cap screwed on tight, push against the tube to force the toothpaste toward the capped end.

RESULTS The toothpaste slowly emerges from the hole and flows down the side of the tube.

WHY? The pressure from your fingers forces the liquid toothpaste out of the opening. Tremendous pressure within the earth forces magma out of cracks or weak spots in the earth's surface. The liquid rock is called magma when it is within the earth, but it is called lava once it reaches the surface. The lava cools and hardens on the surface, forming a mound of rock around the opening. A new layer is added to the mound with each eruption. This layered mound of lava is called a shield volcano.

Squirt!

WASH AWAY

PURPOSE To demonstrate hydraulic mining.

MATERIALS coffee can

        enough small pebbles to line the bottom of the coffee can

        1 cup (250 ml) soil

        spoon

        garden hose with spray nozzle

PROCEDURE

1. Place the pebbles and soil in the can. Mix thoroughly.

2. Place the can outside on the ground.

3. Set the nozzle on the hose at the high-pressure position and direct the stream of water into the can.

4. Continue to spray the water into the can until the overflow water looks clean.

RESULTS The soil is washed out of the can, leaving the pebbles in the bottom of the can.

WHY? Some of the soil dissolves in the water and some of it is light enough to be lifted and carried out of the can by the moving water. The pebbles are too hard to be broken apart by the spraying water. The heavier materials are not lifted by the water, so they remain in the bottom of the can. Rocks that contain metal that can be mined at a profit are called ores. Ore deposits are mined with water. Powerful streams of water are used to wash away the soil surrounding the ore. The rock pieces left are taken to refining plants where pure metals are removed. The process of mining with water is called hydraulic mining.

Wash Away

SHAPING

PURPOSE To demonstrate how land is shaped by abrasion.

MATERIALS fingernail file
6-sided pencil

PROCEDURE

1. Rub the file back and forth across the ridges on the pencil.

2. Observe the surface of the pencil.

RESULTS The ridges of the pencil are cut down.

WHY? The file has a rough, grainy surface. Tiny pieces are cut from the pencil as the file moves back and forth across it. Surfaces can be pitted and polished by sand grains carried by wind. The grains of sand act like the file as they strike and weather surfaces. The wind carries the particles cut away from the surface to other areas. This type of erosion is called abrasion.

WEATHERING

PURPOSE To demonstrate rock weathering due to falling water.

MATERIALS sponge
         sink with a faucet
         bar of soap

PROCEDURE

1. Place the sponge in the sink under the faucet.

2. Put the bar of soap on top of the sponge.

3. For 1 day, use the faucet as usual, allowing the water to hit the center of the soap.

RESULTS An indentation forms in the soap where the water hits it.

WHY? The falling water hits the soap, knocking tiny particles free. Eventually the entire bar of soap will dissolve and wash away. Rocks at the bottom of waterfalls are slowly weathered (broken down into smaller pieces by natural processes). These rocks are much harder than the bar of soap and are not very soluble in water, but eventually the constant force of water hitting their surfaces breaks the rocks apart. The agent of erosion is the running water, which carries the dissolved or broken rock pieces to other areas.

Weathering

**SPEEDY**

PURPOSE To demonstrate how the speed of running water affects the wearing away of soil.

MATERIALS pencil
paper cup
scissors
drinking straw
modeling clay
cookie sheet
ruler
soil
1-gallon (4-liter) plastic jug, filled with tap water

PROCEDURE

1. Use the pencil to make a hole in the side of the paper cup near the bottom.

2. Cut the straw in half and insert one of the pieces into the hole in the cup. Seal around the hole with clay.

3. Lay the cookie sheet on the ground and raise one end about 2 inches (5 cm) by putting soil under it.

4. Cover the sheet with a thin layer of soil. Set the cup on the sheet as shown.

5. Hold your finger over the end of the straw as you fill the cup with water.

6. Release the end of the straw and observe the movement of the water.

7. Repeat steps 4 through 6, raising the end of the sheet about 6 inches (15 cm). Keep the materials for the next experiment, Wander.

RESULTS More soil is washed away when the slope of the cookie sheet is increased.

WHY? As the slope increases, the water flows more quickly. The faster the water moves, the more energy it has, and thus the more soil it pushes forward. The process of being worn away by water is called erosion.

WANDER

PURPOSE To determine why streams are not always straight.

MATERIALS materials from the previous experiment, Speedy
several small rocks

PROCEDURE

1. On the cookie sheet from the previous experiment, push one rock into the soil directly in front of the straw.

2. Continue to fill the cup with water until the running water cuts a definite path in the soil.

3. Change the direction of the stream by placing rocks in the path of the water.

RESULTS A winding stream is cut through the soil.

WHY? Obstacles that cannot be moved by the water change the direction of the stream. Water is routed around the rocks on the cookie sheet, just as it is routed around rocks in streams. Water moves in the direction of least resistance, and the soft soil is easily moved. The shape of waterways is altered by obstacles, such as rocks, and materials that cannot be moved or dissolved easily by the moving water.

GLOSSARY

ANTICLINES Folds in rock layers.

ATMOSPHERE The gases around a planet.

COMPRESSION FORCES Forces pushing toward each other from opposite directions.

DENSITY The scientific way of comparing the "heaviness" of materials.

EVAPORATE To change from a liquid to a gas.

FAULT Where the edges of the tectonic plates come together; crack in the lithosphere where surface rocks have slipped up, down, or sideways.

FRICTION The resistance to motion between two surfaces that are touching each other.

GEYSER An inverted funnel-shaped crack in the earth that periodically throws out jets of hot water and steam.

HYDRAULIC MINING Using powerful streams of water to mine metal.

HYDROSPHERE All of the water on the earth.

IMMISCIBLE LIQUIDS Liquids that are not able to mix together.

INERTIA Resistance to any sudden change in motion or rest.

LAVA Magma that has reached the earth's surface.

LITHOSPHERE The solid outer part of the earth not including the atmosphere or hydrosphere.

MAGMA Molten rock beneath the surface of the earth.

MOLECULE The smallest particle of a substance; made of one or more atoms.

REFLECT To bounce back.

REFRACT To bend.

SHIELD VOLCANO A volcano composed of layers of solidified lava, a wide base, and a large bowl-shaped opening at the top.

STALACTITE A deposit shaped like an icicle, hanging from the roof of a cave.

STALAGMITE A deposit shaped like an upside-down icicle, building up from the floor of a cave.

SYNCLINES Folds in rock layers that curve downward.

TECTONIC PLATES Huge moving pieces of the lithosphere.

TRANSVERSE WAVES Waves that move material up and down or side to side as the energy of the wave moves forward.

For More Information

Canadian Federation of Earth Sciences (CFES)
Department of Earth Sciences
FSS Hall
Room 15025
Ottawa ON K1N 6N5
Canada
(902) 697-7425
Website: http://www.cfes-fcst.ca/

The CFES is a federation of earth science member societies throughout Canada. Read about careers, get your earth science questions answer by an expert with the Ask a Geoscientist! tool, or use their Earth Links to find a multitude of resources about earth science.

National Aeronautics and Space Administration (NASA)
Ames Earth Science Division
NASA Headquarters
300 E. Street SW, Suite 5R30
Washington, DC 20546
(202) 358-0001
Website: http://geo.arc.nasa.gov/

NASA is the premier organization for all things about space and planet Earth! Join the NASA Kids' Club, see photos of Earth from space, and learn more about earth science research.

National Center for Earth and Space Science Education (NCESSE)
P.O. Box 2350
Ellicott City, MD 21041-2350
(301) 395-0770
Website: http://ncesse.org/

The NCESSE creates and oversees national programs addressing STEM education, with a focus on earth and space. Check out Family Science Night, contests, experiment programs, and other community events.

The National Geographic Society
1145 17th Street NW
Washington, DC 20036
(202) 857-7700
Website: http://www.nationalgeographic.com/

The National Geographic Society has been inspiring people to care about the planet since 1888. It is one of the largest nonprofit scientific and educational institutions in the world.

The Society for Science and the Public
Student Science
1719 N Street NW
Washington, DC 20036
(800) 552-4412
Website: https://student.societyforscience.org/

The Society for Science and the Public presents many science project resources, such as science news for students, the latest updates on the Intel Science Talent Search and the Intel International Science and Engineering Fair, and information about cool jobs and doing science.

U.S. Geological Survey (USGS)
12201 Sunrise Valley Drive
Reston, VA 20192
(888) 275-8747
Website: http://www.usgs.gov/

The USGS collects, monitors, analyzes, and provides scientific understanding about natural resource conditions, issues, and problems on the earth.

WEBSITES

Due to the changing nature of Internet links, Rosen Publishing has developed an online list of Web sites related to the subject of this book. This site is updated regularly. Please use this link to access this list:

http://www.rosenlinks.com/JVCW/earth

FOR FURTHER READING

Ardley, Neil. *101 Great Science Experiments*. New York: DK Ltd., 2014.

Ball, Nate. *The Science Unfair* (Alien in My Pocket). New York: Harper, 2014.

Buczynski, Sandy. *Designing a Winning Science Fair Project* (Information Explorer Junior). Ann Arbor, MI: Cherry Lake Publishing, 2014.

Dickmann, Nancy. *Exploring Planet Earth and the Moon* (Spectacular Space Science). New York: Rosen Publishing, 2016.

Henneberg, Susan. *Creating Science Fair Projects with Cool New Digital Tools* (Way Beyond PowerPoint: Making 21st Century Presentations). New York: Rosen Publishing, 2014.

Hyde, Natalie. *Earthquakes, Eruptions, and Other Events that Change Earth* (Earth Processes Close-Up). New York: Crabtree Publishing Co., 2016.

Katirgis, Jane. *Eerie Earthquakes* (Earth's Natural Disasters). New York: Enslow Publishing, Inc., 2016.

Latta, Sara. *All About Earth: Exploring the Planet with Science Projects* (Fact Finders: Discover Earth Science). North Mankato, MN: Capstone Press, 2016.

Margles, Samantha. *Mythbusters Science Fair Book*. New York: Scholastic, 2011.

McGill, Jordan. *Earth Science Fair Projects* (Science Fair Projects). New York: AV2 by Weigl, 2012.

Ruff Ruffman's 44 Favorite Science Activities (Fetch! with Ruff Ruffman). Somerville, MA: Candlewick Press, 2015.

Shea, Therese. *Freaky Weather Stories* (Freaky True Science). New York: Gareth Stevens Publishing, 2016.

Sneideman, Joshua. *Climate Change: Discover How It Impacts Spaceship Earth*. White River Junction, VT: 2015.

Sohn, Emily. *Experiments in Earth Science and Weather* (First Facts: Fun Science). North Mankato, MN: Capstone Press, 2016.

INDEX

A

abrasion, 48
anticlines, 26
atmosphere, 8–9

B

Bang! experiment, 30–31

C

compression forces, 26
continental separation, 20

D

Dripper experiment, 12–13

E

earthquakes, 4, 28–29, 30–31, 32,
    34
earth science, definition of, 4
erosion, 6, 48, 50, 52–53

F

faults, 28–29
Fire Rocks experiment, 42–43
Fossil Dig experiment, 16–17
fossils, 4, 14, 16–17

G

geysers, 22–23
Gulp experiment, 14–15

H

hydraulic mining, 46–47
hydrosphere, 8–9
hypothesis, 7

I

ice, 4, 14
igneous rock, 42–43

J

Jolted experiment, 28–29

L

lava, 42–43, 44
lithosphere, 8–9, 28
lock faults, 28–29

M

magma/molten rock 24–25, 38–39,
    40–41, 42, 44
Megaweight experiment, 8–9
Mid-Atlantic Range, 24–25

O
ores, 46–47

P
petroleum, 4, 18
Pop Top experiment, 22–23
P-waves, 30–31, 32

R
rainbow, 4, 10
Rainbow experiment, 10–11
Riser experiment, 38–39

S
safety, 5
scientific method, 6–7
seismic waves, 30–31, 32
Shaping experiment, 48–49
shield volcano, 44
Shifting experiment, 20–21
Side-to-Side experiment, 34
soil, study of, 4, 6
Speedy experiment, 52–53
Spud Launcher experiment, 40–41
Squeezed experiment, 26–27
Squirt! experiment, 44–45
stalactites, 12–13

stalagmites, 12–13
streams, direction of, 54
sun, 4, 10
S-waves, 32
S-Waves experiment, 32–33
synclines, 26

T
tectonic plates, 28–29
Ticker experiment, 18–19
Tilting experiment, 36–37
tiltmeter, 36–37
transverse wave, 32

V
volcanoes, 4, 36–37, 40–41, 42–43, 44

W
Wander experiment, 54–55
Wash Away experiment, 46–47
Weathering experiment, 50–51
Widening experiment, 24–25